S0-AXI-700

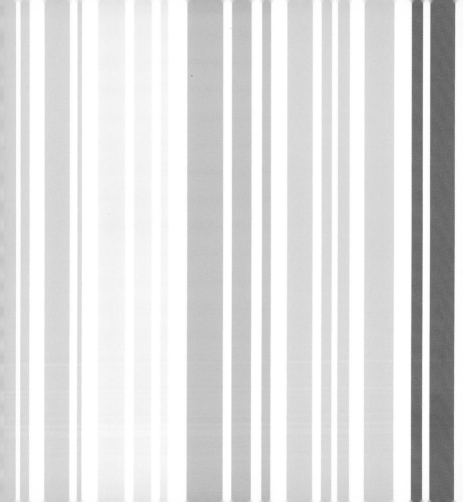

To: ....

From: ....

They BOL and we LOL!

The dog's life certainly has its funny moments.

From puppy play to canine craziness, our pets

amuse us, keep us on our toes, and fill our

hearts with love. Here's a collection of doggy

quips, quotes, and inspiration guaranteed to put

a smile on the face of every dog's best friend.

Dachshunds, ideal dogs for small children, are already stretched and pulled to such a length that the child cannot do much harm.

Robert Benchley

Happiness is a warm puppy.

Charles M. Schulz

Laugh and the world laughs with you. Bark and you have no earthly idea how humans will respond.

Conversations with Dog

My Dog and I

When living seems but little worth
And all things go awry,
I close the door, we journey forth—
My dog and I! . . .
And ere we reach the busy town,
Like birds my troubles fly,
We are two comrades glad of heart—
My dog and I!

Alice J. Cleator

Lord, I know You value this dog whom You've created. May every moment of care I give to my dog reflect Your love for Your creation, and may it bring joy to me and my dog.

Love is patient, love is kind…it is not proud… it is not self-seeking, it is not easily angered, it keeps no record of wrongs.… It always protects, always trusts, always hopes, always perseveres.

1 Corinthians 13:4–5, 7

The great pleasure of a dog is that you may make a fool of yourself with him and not only will he not scold you, but he will make a fool of himself, too.

Samuel Butler

I am a much better person with a dog in my lap.

John O'Hurley

No matter how many toys, bones, and treats you buy, your puppy's favorite chew is still likely to be that sock you've only worn twice or your most treasured pair of shoes.

The reason dogs have so many friends
is because they wag their tails
instead of their tongues.

Unknown

If you get to thinking you're a person
of some influence, try ordering
somebody else's dog around.

Will Rogers

The most affectionate creature in
the world is a wet dog.

Ambrose Bierce

Anybody who doesn't know what
soap tastes like never washed a dog.

Franklin P. Jones

Today I sniffed many dogs' behinds. I celebrate by kissing your face.

Rover

If you think dogs can't count, try putting three dog biscuits in your pocket and then giving Fido only two of them.

Phil Pastoret

The dog has got more fun out of man than man has got out of the dog for the clearly demonstrable reason that man is the more laughable of the two animals.

James Thurber

A door is what a dog
is perpetually on the
wrong side of.

Ogden Nash

Thank You, Lord, for the joys of having a dog. Help me to find enough time to play with him, walk him, and care for him. May he not only be my best friend; may I be his.

Give, and it will be given to you. A good measure, pressed down, shaken together and running over.

Luke 6:38

Why do dachshunds wear their ears inside out?

P. G. Wodehouse

Dachshund: A half-a-dog high and a dog-and-a-half long.

Henry Louis Mencken

One dog barks at something,
the rest bark at him.

Chinese Proverb

Dogs come when they're called.

Cats take a message and get back to you.

Mary Bly

Eat a live toad first thing in the morning and nothing worse will happen to you the rest of the day.

Found Out the Hard Way by Rover

Animal-Shelter Sign:
CHILDREN LEFT UNATTENDED WILL
BE GIVEN A PUPPY OR KITTEN

Every puppy should have a boy.

Erma Bombeck

I used to look at [my dog] Smokey and think, "If you were a little smarter you could tell me what you were thinking," and he'd look at me like he was saying, "If you were a little smarter, I wouldn't have to."

Fred Jungclaus

The God who made giraffes, a baby's fingernails, a puppy's tail, a crookneck squash, the bobwhite's call, and a young girl's giggle has a sense of humor. Make no mistake about that.

Catherine Marshall

Let sleeping dogs lie—
unless you need to roll over in bed at 3 a.m.

Bought a three-legged dog once.
Had to—he was 25 percent off.
Named him "Tripawd."

Dr. Kenneth Fogelberg

Help me, Lord, to sometimes see life through my dog's eyes. May I appreciate the joy of greeting someone I love and delight in the cool morning breeze as we take a long walk together.

Clothe yourselves with compassion, kindness, humility, gentleness and patience.

Colossians 3:12

Breed a boxer with a German shorthair, you get a boxershorts. A dog never seen in public.
Good Dog! Magazine

I don't eat anything that a dog won't eat. Like sushi. Ever see a dog eat sushi? He just sniffs it and says, "I don't think so." And this is an animal that licks between its legs and sniffs fire hydrants.
Billiam Coronel

You may have a dog that won't sit up,
roll over, or even cook breakfast,
not because she's too stupid to learn how
but because she's too smart to bother.
Rick Horowitz

Some of my best leading men have
been dogs and horses.
Elizabeth Taylor

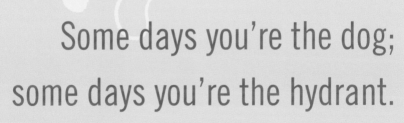

Some days you're the dog;
some days you're the hydrant.

Unknown

If you can look at a dog and not feel vicarious excitement and affection, you must be a cat.

Unknown

I bought a dog. . .named him Stay. It's fun to call him: "Come here, Stay! Come here, Stay!" He went insane.

Steven Wright

I wonder if other dogs think poodles are members of a weird religious cult.

Rita Rudner

My goal in life is to be as good a person as my dog thinks I am.

Unknown

Outside of a dog, a book is a man's best friend. Inside a dog, it's too dark to read anyhow.

What you call "begging" I call "just sitting here patiently waiting till you give me what I want."

Butch

Lord, You've helped me appreciate how wondrously You've made the dog. Out of all the animals You made, this one was designed as my special companion and friend. Thank You.

"This is the sign of the covenant I am making between me and you and every living creature.... Whenever the rainbow appears in the clouds, I will see it and remember the everlasting covenant between God and all living creatures of every kind on the earth."

Genesis 9:12, 16

There are all sorts of cute puppy dogs, but it doesn't stop people from going out and buying Dobermans.

Angus Young

There is no psychiatrist in the world like a puppy licking your face.

Ben Williams

Study hard, and you might grow up to be president. But let's face it: Even then, you'll never make as much money as your dog.

George H. W. Bush

Any man who does not like dogs and want them about does not deserve to be in the White House.

Calvin Coolidge

Why own a dog?
There's a danger you know.
You can't own just one,
for the craving will grow.
There's no doubt they're addictive,
wherein lies the danger.
While living with lots,
you'll grow poorer and stranger.

Unknown

Bulldogs are adorable, with faces like toads that have been sat on.

Colette

Dogs feel very strongly that they should always go with you in the car, in case the need should arise for them to bark violently at nothing right in your ear.

Dave Barry

I have a little brindle dog,
Seal-brown from tail to head.
His name I guess is Theodore,
But I just call him Ted. . . .

He plays around about the house,
As good as he can be,
He don't seem like a little dog,
He's just like folks to me.

Maxine Anna Buck

Labradors are lousy watchdogs. They usually bark when there is a stranger about, but it is an expression of unmitigated joy at the chance to meet somebody new, not a warning.

Norman Strung

Cat's Motto: No matter what you've done wrong, always try to make it look like the dog did it.

Unknown

Beware of the man who does not talk, and the dog that does not bark.

Cheyenne Proverb

I just don't understand what is so bad about drinking out of the toilet. To me it's a self-serve water bowl!

Fido

Thank You, Lord, for my lively little pup. Remind me that these days of puppyhood are short. Give me large doses of patience and love, along with enough determination to train her for a lifetime.

And God said, "Let the land produce living creatures according to their kinds...." And it was so.... And God saw that it was good.

Genesis 1:24–25

I'll be good, really! pleaded the dog's eyes. You welcome him into your home, shower him with affection, train him in your ways. In time, he finally feels loved. One day he empties the trash can on your floor, breaks into the dog treats, and chews six rolls of toilet paper. Congratulations, you've bonded!

[Being a parent] is tough.
If you just want a wonderful
little creature to love,
you can get a puppy.

Barbara Walters

Leash: A long, web-like device that allows a dog to control his human and pull her in the opposite direction of where she would otherwise go.

There are two kinds of dog toys: the one that lasts for years because your dog loves it so much she treats it gently, and the one that is so vigorously chewed, it only lasts an hour. Who's to say which gives more enjoyment?

As much as any animal on earth, dogs express emotions as purely and clearly as a five-year-old child, and surely that's part of why we love them so much.

Patricia B. McConnell

Every boy who has a dog should also have a mother, so the dog won't starve.

Unknown

If your dog is fat, you're not getting enough exercise.

Unknown

I'm not fat, I'm fluffy! Now give me treats!

Butch

I've never been able to fully experience the joy of food. Scarfing it out of the bowl as fast as I can seems like the best option to me.

Rover

No matter how big the dog bowl is, a long-eared, deep-flewed dog never keeps water inside the bowl. Instead he shares it with the floors and walls. If he shakes his head, his humans may even find themselves cleaning the ceiling.

Thank You, Lord, for giving me a dog who reminds me of the joy in life. When people depress me with bad news, my dog points out that there's still reason to remain cheerful: we still have each other and a good game of ball.

A cheerful heart is good medicine.
Proverbs 17:22

A Pekingese is not a pet dog; he is an undersized lion.

A. A. Milne

[Mungo] was a medium-sized dog, nothing special, a hound of some sort; the kind you'd pick out at the shelter to adopt, flop-eared, tan-and-white coat, immediately likable; the kind of dog you itched to scratch between the ears.

Martha Grimes

A man running for office puts me in mind of a dog that's lost—he smells everybody he meets and wags himself all over.

Josh Billings

The more I come to know men,
the more I come to admire the dog.

A. Toussenel

When I came to live with you,
I wasn't impressed with the size of
your home. All I cared about was the
size of your heart.

Rover

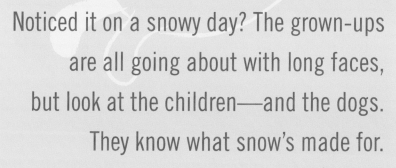

Noticed it on a snowy day? The grown-ups
are all going about with long faces,
but look at the children—and the dogs.
They know what snow's made for.

C. S. Lewis

I really love the new couch.
Its dark color really helps me see
how much I am shedding.

Fido

In times of joy, all of us wished we
possessed a tail we could wag.

W. H. Auden

Lord, thank You for the deep dog-human bond. May people who have lost their beloved companions be comforted by Your deep love and know that not one bit of fur was uncounted by You.

The entire law is fulfilled in keeping this one command: "Love your neighbor as yourself."
Galatians 5:14

All dogs are opportunists. That's important to remember when you try to teach your puppy the rules of the house.
John Ross and Barbara McKinney

Those who will play with cats must expect to be scratched.
Miguel de Cervantes

I've caught more ills from people sneezing over me and giving me virus infections than from kissing dogs.

Barbara Woodhouse

Dog clothes aren't okay.
I don't care how cute you think
they are. They're unnatural
(and hilarious to other dogs).

Butch

I sometimes think I'd rather be a dog and bay at the moon than stay in the Senate another six years and listen to it.

Senator John Sharp Williams

Whoever loveth me, loveth my hound.

Thomas More

Dogs laugh, but they laugh with their tails.

Max Eastman

I'm so excited my whole body's wagging!

Butch

Folks will know how large your soul is by the way you treat a dog.

Charles F. Doran

My little old dog:
a heartbeat at my feet.

Edith Wharton

Please take the cone off.
I promise I won't lick it or bite
it. Dog's honor. How can you say
no to these puppy dog eyes?

Fido

Lord, to many people I know this is "just a dog." But she is Your creation, designed with a sensitive nose, fast legs, and a wide-open heart. Thank You for this special gift You've given me. May she never be "just a dog" to me.

"In his hand is the life of every creature and the breath of all mankind."

Job 12: 10